Selections From
CHANGE THE WORLD

SELECTIONS FROM CHANGE THE WORLD

This book is printed on acid-free paper.

ISBN 978-1-426-71176-3

Unless otherwise indicated, scripture quotations are taken from the
Holy Bible, TODAY'S NEW INTERNATIONAL VERSION®. Copyright
© 2001, 2005 International Bible Society. All rights reserved throughout
the world. Used by permission of the International Bible Society.

Verses marked (NRSV) are taken from the New Revised Standard Ver-
sion of the Bible, copyright 1989, Division of Christian Education of the
National Council of the Churches of Christ in the United States of
America. Used by permission. All rights reserved.

Verses marked (KJV) are taken from the King James or Authorized Ver-
sion of the Bible.

10 11 12 13 14 15 16 17 18 19—10 9 8 7 6 5 4 3 2 1
MANUFACTURED IN THE UNITED STATES OF AMERICA

Foreword

Mike's book *Change the World*, his work, and the ministry of Ginghamsburg United Methodist Church are a rallying cry for, as Mike says, "rediscovering and reclaiming the message and mission of Jesus." I've said before that each generation of believers must decide whether their Christianity will have anything to do with Jesus. That challenge faces churches, big and small alike, across the country and the world each and every day. Whether or not what they do, how they spend their time, and use their resources will have anything to do with Jesus.

Mike's challenge is simple and direct: "Quit worrying about getting people into your church and start finding opportunities to move the people who are already there out into God's service." It is a challenge that, if we pick it up, will not only change our churches but also transform the world.

Jim Wallis

Recovering the Message and Mission of Jesus

The mandate for Jesus' followers is clear. The leader of our movement defined the parameters of our mission in his inaugural message at Nazareth:

> The Spirit of the Lord is on me, because he has anointed me to proclaim good news to the poor. He has sent me to proclaim freedom for the prisoners and recovery of sight for the blind, to set the oppressed free, to proclaim the year of the Lord's favor. (Luke 4:18-19, quoting Isa 61:1-2)

He has already given us the action items that will be the measures of evaluation on God's final exam:

> I was hungry and you gave me something to eat . . . thirsty and you gave me something to drink . . . a stranger and you invited me in, I needed clothes and you clothed me . . . sick and you looked after me . . . in prison and you came to visit me. . . . Truly I tell you, whatever you did for one of the least of these brothers and sisters of mine, you did for me. (Matt 25:35-40)

The gospel is good news for the poor. If it is not working to benefit the poor and oppressed, then it is not the gospel! Jesus calls his followers to a lifestyle of sacrificial mission, giving ourselves with him for God's redemptive work in the world.

Something Is Not Working

David Kinnaman and Gabe Lyons's work, *Un-christian: What a New Generation Really Thinks about Christianity*, should be a jolting wake-up call for the church.

Kinnaman and Lyons said, "The image of the Christian faith has suffered a major setback. Our most recent data show that young outsiders have lost much of their respect for the Christian faith. These days nearly two out of every five young outsiders (38 percent) claim to have a bad impression of present-day Christianity." The research reveals that the three most widely held perceptions of the Christian church are that it is (1) antihomosexual (an image held by 91 percent of sixteen- to nineteen-year-old outsiders); (2) judgmental (87 percent); and (3) hypocritical (85 percent). [1]

The business of the church is to engage and empower disciples of Jesus in meeting the needs and closing the gaps of disparities for the least of these. The world will see the relevancy of the gospel when the people of Jesus fully embrace and live the biblical mandate to love like Jesus. John Wesley called it the demonstration of "social holiness." The church too often suffers from a numbers neurosis. Let's quit worrying about numbers in the pews and begin to be the hands and feet of Jesus in our homes, our communities, and the outermost places of the world. It is time for the church to rediscover and reclaim the message and mission of Jesus!

Are We Missional?

"All great missionary movements begin at the fringes of the church, among the poor and the marginalized, and seldom, if ever, at the center." —Alan Hirsch

Jesus' mission centers on three biblical mandates that define the mission operative for the church.

1. The Great Requirement

> He has shown all you people what is good. And what does the LORD require of you? To act justly and to love mercy and to walk humbly with your God. (Mic 6:8)

We need to look at these actions individually.

Justice. We are called to *do* justice and not just to believe in justice or study justice. You have power with God by your actions toward people, especially the poor and marginalized. Justice is a core biblical theme:

The LORD is known by his acts of justice. (Ps 9:16)

Righteousness and justice are the foundation of your throne. (Ps 89:14)

Follow justice and justice alone, so that you may live and possess the land the LORD your God is giving you. (Deut 16:20)

The LORD works righteousness
and justice for all the oppressed. (Ps 103:6)

Mercy. Participants of the missional church will be both activists for justice and living demonstrations of God's mercy. Mercy is closely related to grace—receiving what one doesn't deserve or hasn't earned. Mercy is the generous demonstration of indescribable grace! The missional church is actively and practically demonstrating God's mercy through ministries that provide daily life necessities in the communities where they are located.

Humility. Mission evangelism differs from attraction in the sense that it moves out and serves others regardless of cultural, political, moral, or creedal differences. It serves without expectation of return or self-gain. This is what it means to walk humbly with God. It is not about us or for us. It's about serving Jesus in other people: "For I was hungry and you gave me something to eat . . ."

2. The Great Commandment

> My command is this: Love each other as I have loved you. Greater love has no one than this: to lay down one's life for one's friends. (John 15:12-13)

The Jesus follower cannot live this mandate and stay in comfortable places. The tremendous work of rehabilitation in the aftermath of Hurricane Katrina is just one example of Jesus followers venturing into uncomfortable places to act in love for people they've never met. Volunteers from Ginghamsburg spend Thanksgiving and Christmas breaks lifting the hopes and restoring the residences of those who have been ripped off by insurance companies and contractors. The church is the largest nongovernment/nonprofit social agency in the United States. Would your community be different if your church closed its doors tomorrow?

3. The Great Commission

> All authority in heaven and earth has been given to me. Therefore go and make disciples of all nations, baptizing them in the name of the Father and of the Son and of the Holy Spirit, and teaching them to obey everything I have commanded you. (Matt 28:18-20)

Mission evangelism serves without expectation, honoring all people as children who are created in the image of God. We work outside the walls, structures, barriers, and limitations of the institution to promote God's justice through the demonstration of generous and practical services of mercy.

You don't need to have hundreds of people in your church to be actively and faithfully serving Jesus' mission. Churches are doing it with fewer than fifteen! Where do you see a great need in your community or the world? Quit worrying about getting people into your church, and start finding opportunities to move the people who are already there out into God's service. Religion that honors God is religion with feet.

Are We Inclusive?

"I like your Christ, I do not like your Christians. Your Christians are so unlike your Christ." —Mohandas Gandhi

Many of us in the church seek out places of worship that tend to embrace our personal political persuasions, excluding anyone from "true" fellowship who doesn't see eye to eye. The "Christian" extreme radio pundits of the airwaves proclaim God's anointed and defame the heretical. This spirit of disdain and exclusion prevents many outsiders from experiencing the resurrected Christ and drives some seekers from the church.

Followers of Jesus are committed to relationships of integrity and truth. But somewhere along the way, we have lost sight of the spirit of the one who embodies truth. Like the Pharisees of Jesus' day, we may know the letter of the law while missing the spirit of God's intent. Given the exclusivity with which many Christians interpret Christ's message, you can begin to understand why there is such indifference and even hostility toward the gospel by those outside the church.

All Scripture must be interpreted through and in the spirit of Jesus. When you read any passage, you must ask yourself, *How is this like God who is revealed in Jesus?*

God is fully revealed in Jesus. Jesus clarified the moral character of God and the window through which we must do biblical interpretation:

> You have heard that it was said, "Eye for eye, and tooth for tooth." But I tell you, do not resist an evil person. If anyone slaps you on the right cheek, turn to them the other cheek also. . . . You have heard that it was said, "Love your neighbor and hate your enemy." But I tell you, love your enemies and pray for those who persecute you, that you may be children of your Father in heaven. (Matt 5:38-39, 43-45)

The way of Jesus is a higher way. His followers willfully choose life over condemnation. After the woman was caught in the act of adultery, the teachers of the Law and Pharisees took her to Jesus and demanded that she be given the justice that the law of Moses commanded (see John 8:2-11). How many people has the church stoned through the ages in the name of God, using the letter but not the spirit of the word? How many are we still stoning? Jesus didn't follow the letter of the Law. He fulfilled the spirit of the Law.

Have you ever been burned by toxic religion or religious people? *Toxic* means "deadly." It affects our understanding of who God is. Toxic religion causes us to perceive God as being critical, unapproachable, and inaccessible. Most people I know believe in God but really struggle with the idea that God believes in them. Because of the way people in the church have treated them in the past, they are convinced that God has rejected them too.

"Our Father who art . . ." These words contain possibly the most revolutionary understanding about God that Jesus brought into the world. God is our Father! God is not exclusive to one tribe or nation, but God is Father of all nations, tribes, and peoples on the earth. It is significant that on the day of Pentecost (the birthday of the church), the spirit of God was not given until God-fearing people were gathered from "every nation under heaven" (see Acts 2). The list is truly amazing in its inclusivity. God was even inclusive in language. Everyone present heard the word in his or her native tongue. None was left out. The first Christians were Jews. And guess what? Arabs were also invited to the party. Even the Cretans are mentioned, and they were on the top of everyone's list of folks you never want to date your children or to move in next door! God truly wants us to be one big, happy family.

Are We Growing Disciples?

"The quality of the church's leadership is directly proportional to the quality of discipleship. If we fail in the area of making disciples, we should not be surprised if we fail in the area of leadership development."
—*Alan Hirsch*

The early Christian church was an unofficial movement that existed in tension with the established religious institution and the Roman state. It lacked the institutional structures, such as a credentialed priesthood and buildings, which would give it the validation of an official religion. It was driven by a passionate belief that a revolutionary leader had come to establish a countercultural kingdom on earth.

We can spend a whole lifetime in the construction of a ministry that has nothing to do with Christ's commission, despite giving the appearance of success. Don't get distracted in building the church instead of disciples. It can easily become a distraction in challenging economic times. Jesus said, "I will build my church, and the gates of death will not overcome it" (Matt 16:18). Church building is his job. Then what's ours? "Go and make disciples!"

Disciples model the message. They replicate the life and mission of Jesus in the world. Disciples operate out of a sense of calling that is spiritually motivated. Disciples do not need to be coerced. Their commitment is active and spiritually sustained. Like the prophets and saints who have gone before them, disciples have heard the voice of God asking: "Whom shall I send? And who will go for us?" They have willfully responded: "Here am I. Send me!" (Isa 6:8).

Understanding your life purpose is discovering why you are alive and knowing the contribution that you want to leave behind. Some people confuse life purpose with goals. Life purpose is not to be confused with a job. You can lose your job, but you can't lose your life mission.

Will We Focus Our Resources on Mission?

In the 1990s, many of us were talking about the 24/7 church—the church that ran a complex array of programming seven days a week, twenty-four hours a day. The missional church that is engaging its community and world in the places of real need today will not waste time and resources fueling complex organizational structures and programs. Less is more! The focus will be given to the fundamentals of community, discipleship, and mission.

We need to focus our best strategies on new church places where the majority of people live and work. Ginghamsburg's Fort McKinley campus is one church restart into which we are pouring our energy and resources. The highly transient Fort McKinley neighborhood is comprised of 65 to 70 percent rental properties. Residents do not know their neighbors. Folks fail to pay their rent and move every three to six months. Now this sounds exactly like the place where the church needs to be!

The original Fort McKinley United Methodist church was all white, using European worship styles in a neighborhood that was primarily African American. We sent a transition team in November 2007. I asked eighty members from Ginghamsburg to become urban missionaries and make the Fort McKinley campus their place of worship and service.

By pouring our energy into the Fort McKinley community, we have been able to meet an enormous number of real, felt needs among struggling people. We are meeting immediate physical needs through food pantries, a grocery co-op, a senior lunch program, and free community meals four days a week. Our gently used clothing and furniture stores and car and medical supply ministries seek to provide urgent care. Some funds are available to help clients with utility bills.

For children, we offer a tutoring program in the elementary school three blocks away, and an after-school clubhouse tutor/mentor program for at-risk elementary children that meets four afternoons each week. We have adopted Belle Haven Elementary School in the Fort McKinley neighborhood, ensuring that each teacher has a volunteer assistant (which allows for more individual student attention), supporting all of Belle Haven's special events such as perfect attendance luncheons, field days, festivals, and art shows—all ways to expand students' horizons and provide for activities that the recession-riddled urban public tax system can't support. Dayton City Schools have consistently been ranked at the bottom of Ohio school districts. Belle Haven students were scoring in the bottom third among their peers in the Dayton district. In just three years, Belle Haven went from an evaluation of "academic emergency" to "continuous improvement."

Social programs like these are centered in the heart of the holistic gospel of Jesus Christ. There cannot be personal holiness apart from social holiness, and social holiness cannot be sustained apart from a personal relationship with God. The goal of all of our work is to connect people to the liberating love of Jesus and to empower folks to rise out of the malaise of poverty. We are meeting real spiritual needs through two Sunday morning worship opportunities, Sunday morning classes for all ages that focus on life skills and discipleship, a Sunday evening worship service for people in recovery, and a Tuesday evening Bible study. We have found that breakfast has been a quick way to generate worship attendance at Fort McKinley, so there is a free breakfast complete with omelets made to order and pancakes to die for. There is no pressure—or strings attached—to attend. Relationship building between our urban missionaries and neighborhood folk is extremely strategic and beneficial during these meals. Didn't Jesus' disciples recognize the risen Lord when they broke bread together? Through the development of friendships, relevant music, and word, people eventually move from the dining room to the living room of fellowship!

If Ginghamsburg had poured its resources into expanding our current facilities in our main location, we would not have been able to do Christ's work in this other area of our city. By multiplying rather than expanding, we can make disciples who revitalize communities in need. The leadership team at Ginghamsburg Church is currently studying the demographics of other blighted urban neighborhoods in the city, looking at dying churches, and strategically planning our next restart.

Theology of Space: Tent or Temple?

Growing churches inevitably face space constraints. With growth comes the dilemma to build or not to build, where to build, and what to build? This is when we must honestly wrestle with the issue of theology of space. Buildings define our ministry and values. They also create a certain permanence that tends to become restrictive with demographic and culture shifts. Much of The United Methodist Church's ministry has been limited by the fact that more than 70 percent of our church facilities are located in small towns and rural areas where only 16 percent of the U.S. population lives. The permanence of our nineteenth- and twentieth-century capital assets has us out of position for twenty-first-century mission. Our brittle wineskins cannot hold new wine! Why are we reluctant to commit to new wineskins? We have assigned sacred value to our physical facilities, and we can't let go. Buildings are not sacred—people are sacred! We need to let go of buildings and invest in the world that God loves and for whom Jesus died.

Minimizing bricks and mortar means making sacrifices in the church budget and operations, but maximizing mission also means teaching disciples to make sacrifices in their personal budget and lifestyle, living simply so that others may simply live.

Christmas Is Not Your Birthday

Christmas Day has become the number one self-focused consumer day in America. The indicator of its economic success is determined by the day after Thanksgiving sales, appropriately named Black Friday.

Since 2004, the folks at Ginghamsburg have tried to reframe the message and mission of Christmas as being Christ's birthday and to do what honors him on the occasion of his birth. Christmas is not about us! We have chosen to make the Advent season a focus on the Sudan Project and to sacrificially raise the needed funds for the coming year. We spend minimally on our families so that we can give sacrificially for the needs of people in Darfur. We build the Christmas Eve celebrations around this mission focus.

The traditional Christmas that we have grown up with is about a feel-good, insulated, holly-jolly Santa

Claus Jesus who leaves us isolated from the needs of the world. We are detached from the servant Son of God who would not be exempt or insulated from pain, suffering, or death. Jesus experienced the injustice and unfairness of life in its extremes when he lived with his family as refugees in Africa to escape the Judean genocide. He was executed as a criminal of the state around the age of thirty-three. So will someone please tell me: Where is the disconnect between Jesus' birthday, refugees, genocide, and Africa?

The contemporary church has tended to err either by denying the validity of the uniqueness of Jesus and the historicity of his resurrection or by retreating into a form of the ancient cult of Gnosticism, which regards God's creation as inherently evil and seeks refuge in a future disembodied heaven. The Bible teaches not about some form of disembodied heaven after death, but about the resurrection of the body and the creation of a new heaven and earth. God has not abandoned the planet or the people in it. God is constantly restoring, renewing, redeeming, and resurrecting. The people of Jesus are called to be a counterculture community who are demonstrating heaven's purpose on earth.

Renewals and reformation are never born out of timidity. I love to "double dare" women and to men to live beyond the limits of reason and to grab hold of God's possibilities through limitless faith.

Will We Be Courageous?

"Courage is being scared to death and saddling up anyway." — John Wayne

God calls his people to act courageously in times of chaos. The children of God had allowed the paralysis of fear to turn what should have been an exodus trip of a few months into a forty-year waste of a lifetime for a whole generation. When Joshua was preparing to lead the new generation into the land of God's promise, here is what God said to him:

> Be strong and courageous; for you shall put this people in possession of the land that I swore to their ancestors to give them. Only be strong and very courageous, being careful to act in accordance with all the law that my servant Moses commanded you; do not turn from it to the right hand or to the left, so that you may be successful wherever you go. (Josh 1:6-7, NRSV)

The first words of Easter morning from the lips of our resurrected and reigning Lord were, "Do not be afraid." Faith is not the absence of fear. Faith is feeling the fear and then acting on the promises and purpose of God anyway. Faith is the proactive response, in spite of those feelings and uncertainties, to the mandates of heaven.

Faith is not the absence of doubt or fear. Faith is acting on God's word in spite of!

I find four directives for faith, given by Jesus after his resurrection, to be extremely practical in chaotic times of uncertainty (see Matt 28).

1. Don't let fear determine your actions. God is the God of abundance, love, life, and provision. Not even death can deny God's redemptive plan. No circumstance can change the promise or purposes of God! Life is a choice. We choose our life situation. God said, "I have set before you life and death, blessings and curses. Now choose life, so that you and your children may live" (Deut 30:19). To experience life, you must take risks.

2. Recognize holy ground. I have discovered that the fruit of a person's life work rise to the level of his or her expectations. "As he thinketh in his heart, so is he" (Prov 23:7, KJV). You don't need different circumstances, new surroundings, or more resources. You are in God's place, in God's time. Wherever you are, God is.

3. Serve God's purpose in others. Jesus stated, "I give you a new commandment, that you love one another. Just as I have loved you, you also should love one another. By this everyone will know that you are my disciples, if you have love for one another" (John 13:34-35, NRSV). How are you serving Jesus by serving others, especially those on the margins of society?

Praise God for the people of God who stand in courage and speak to evil in Jesus' name, "Not on our watch!"

God never intended for people to sit around and wait for heaven. Jesus calls us from our complacency and places of comfort to go into all the world and make disciples. This calling is not just for professional clergy but also for every person who responds to Jesus' invitation, "Follow me!" How can we change the world? By equipping disciples in small out-of-the-way places who will go into the world and serve God's purpose in others.

4. Focus forward. Jesus is always moving ahead of the church into the future. Don't look back. God's best days are before us. God's purpose is in front of us—never behind.

Helping people see the simple truth of Jesus' purpose. Reconnecting women and men to the basic message and mission of Jesus. This is when real change begins in a local church. And this Holy Spirit-empowered change becomes a contagion that spreads through communities and ultimately the world!

NOTES

[1] David Kinnaman and Gabe Lyons, *Unchristian: What a New Generation Really Thinks about Christianity* (Grand Rapids: Baker Books, 2007), 24, 27.

RETHINK
CHURCH

What if we rethink church...not in terms of what it is, but what it could be?

Rethink Church is a movement designed to remind those inside and outside of faith communities that church is not just a place we go, but something we do. Created by the people of The United Methodist Church, it presents doorways to spirituality – everything from global health initiatives to community outreach programs and church recreation leagues.

Resources for United Methodist congregations, conferences and for those looking for a way to change the world visit:
www.rethinkchurch.org